Charlie Catches A Bee

A Child's Read-Aloud Story Book

Written by

Charles Albert Haigh

For my amazing, ever curious
grandchildren...
Katey, Rowan, Juli, Ella, and Teagun...

And for curious children everywhere...
May your sense of wonder and love of
nature never cease...

Author's note...

"Charlie Catches A Bee" was intended from the start as an 'illustrated' child's read-aloud story book. Perhaps a reader knows of a talented artist/illustrator willing to undertake such a project?

I

Charlie loved playing outdoors in the summertime.

Summertime was barefoot time.

Summertime was run and splash in puddles time.

Summertime was feeling cool green clover between your toes time.

Summertime was also the time Charlie caught a bee.

II

Charlie was four years old.

The time was the 1940s, after World War II had ended.

Charlie lived in a small Southern town with his mother and father.

They lived in a two-story house surrounded by a big yard.

The yard was covered by patches of cool green clover with large white blossoms.

The clover attracted honey bees who sipped sweet nectar from the blossoms.

When a bee landed on a blossom to sip nectar, pollen from the plant collected on the bee's hind legs.

When the bee landed on another blossom to sip nectar, pollen fell onto the plant, fertilizing it.

Back in their hive, bees turned clover nectar into thick, sweet honey.

III

Charlie loved watching bees fly from blossom to blossom.

He was too young to understand how bees turn nectar into honey or pollinate plants by landing on them.

He just loved lying on his tummy in the clover, making crude drawings of bees on a notepad as they busily buzzed from blossom to blossom.

IV

One day, Charlie thought it would be fun to catch a bee so he could see it better.

He felt if he could see it better, he could draw it better.

He went to a shed behind the house and found a glass jar with a metal lid.

He went back to the clover field and patiently waited on his knees for a bee to land on a nearby blossom.

Sure enough, a while later, a bee landed on the blossom.

Holding the glass jar in one hand and the metal lid in the other, Charlie quickly trapped the bee inside the jar.

He screwed the lid on tight to keep the bee inside.

The bee buzzed angrily around inside the jar as it tried to get out.

Excited over his catch, Charlie ran toward the house.

He wanted to show his mom the bee he had caught.

V

Charlie's mom was in the kitchen baking cakes and cookies for a neighborhood bake sale.

Holding the jar with the bee trapped inside, Charlie ran into the kitchen.

"Look, mom!" he cried. "I caught a bee in a jar!"

Charlie's mom knew how curious he was about such things.

She knew he liked to draw pictures of bugs, insects and small animals he saw while playing in the yard.

She took the jar and looked at the angry bee inside.

"You certainly did, Charlie," she said. "What a beautiful bee!"

She smiled and handed the jar back to Charlie. "Now you have to set it free."

"But why, mom?" Charlie cried. "Why can't I keep the bee and draw pictures of it?"

"Because the bee will die in this jar," Charlie's mom patiently explained.

She showed Charlie a jar of clover honey she was using in her baking.

"Bees make honey," she told him, "and this bee wants to go back to the hive to make more honey."

She pointed out the window at the fields of clover surrounding the house. "Bees also pollinate plants like clover by landing on them."

She patted Charlie gently on the head, then tousled his hair. "You need to take the bee outside and let it go, okay?"

"Okay, mom," Charlie sadly replied.

He walked slowly back outside with the jar.

VI

In the yard, Charlie loosened the lid and started to free the bee.

Then he looked back at the house to see if his mom was watching. She was nowhere in sight.

Charlie screwed the lid back on the jar.

He looked at the bee inside the jar.

"I'll just draw some pictures of you," he whispered to the bee. "Then I'll let you go, okay?"

The bee buzzed angrily around inside the jar.

VII

Charlie entered the shed with the jar and closed the door.

He put the jar on a shelf under the window, in bright sunlight.

"Let me get some paper and a pencil, okay?" Charlie said to the bee.

The bee buzzed angrily around inside the jar, though not as angrily as before. It seemed to be growing tired.

Charlie took a pencil and pad of paper from a drawer.

He sat on a wooden stool and stared at the bee for a while.

Turning the jar this way and that, he made rough drawings of the bee from different angles.

VIII

After a while, Charlie grew tired of drawing the bee.

The bee had stopped buzzing angrily around inside the jar. It crawled slowly around the bottom of the jar, in bright sunlight.

"I'll just play outside a while," Charlie told the bee. "Then I'll let you go, okay?"

Charlie went outside to play. He closed the door to the shed.

IX

A while later, Charlie returned to the shed.

He entered and picked up the jar with the bee inside.

"I'll let you go now, okay?" he said to the bee.

The bee didn't move.

Charlie shook the jar.

The bee still didn't move. It lay still at the bottom of the jar.

Charlie shook the jar once more. The bee still didn't move.

Charlie sighed. His shoulders slumped and his head drooped low. He knew something bad had happened.

He took the jar outside the shed.

X

Still busy in the kitchen, Charlie's mom glanced out the window.

She saw Charlie leave the shed carrying the jar.

She saw his slumped shoulders and head held low.

She saw him remove the lid from the jar and dump the dead bee into the grass.

She saw Charlie stand still for a while, staring at the dead bee.

She saw him put the lid back on the jar, then slowly return to the shed and close the door.

XI

Charlie's mom knew he already felt badly about what had happened to the bee. She was sad that Charlie had disobeyed her, but hoped he had learned from his mistake. She decided not to say anything to Charlie about the bee.

XII

The following Saturday was hot and humid, as it normally is in the South in the summer.

Charlie's mom made a picnic lunch for Charlie, his dad and herself.

After they finished eating, Charlie's mom and dad sat in a large swing in the shade of a tree.

While swinging, they sipped glasses of cold iced tea, sweetened with honey, and nibbled on homemade peanut butter and honey cookies.

XIII

Barefoot as usual, Charlie knelt in a nearby patch of clover, watching the bees.

He finished a cookie and washed it down with cold, sweet tea.

Suddenly, a bee landed on the rim of Charlie's empty glass. The bee was attracted by the honey Charlie's mom used to sweeten the tea.

Without thinking, Charlie quickly clamped his hand over the glass, trapping the bee inside.

The bee buzzed angrily around inside the glass.

Excited, Charlie leapt to his feet and ran toward his mom and dad.

He held the glass upside down with the palm of his hand blocking the bottom.

The angry bee landed on Charlie's open palm.

"Mom! Dad! I caught a bee!" Charlie cried.

Before Charlie's mom or dad could say a word, the trapped bee stung Charlie's open palm.

Charlie screamed and dropped the glass.

"It stung me! The bee stung me!" Charlie cried in pain.

"I'll get some ice," Charlie's dad said, and ran toward the picnic table.

Charlie's mom took his hand in hers and looked at it.

The bee had flown away, but the bee's stinger and poison sac stuck to Charlie's palm.

Charlie's mom scraped the stinger and poison sac away with a fingernail.

Charlie's palm was swollen and red.

His dad returned with a glass of ice.

"It hurts, mom! It hurts so bad!" Charlie cried, tears streaming down his cheeks.

Charlie's mom put some ice on the swollen area in the middle of his palm.

"I know, sweetheart. The ice will make it better," she assured him, wiping tears from his cheeks.

"Why did the bee leave the stinger in my hand?" Charlie cried.

"The stinger has barbs on it, son. That's why it stuck to you," his dad explained.

Charlie's mom looked out over the field of clover.

"When a bee stings you, Charlie, part of the bee stays with the stinger. The bee that stung you flew off somewhere to die."

Charlie felt badly about this.

He remembered the bee that died in the jar a few days earlier.

He sighed heavily. His head hung lower. His shoulders slumped.

Charlie's dad took a clean handkerchief from his pocket. He wrapped the handkerchief around Charlie's hand to hold ice on the swollen area.

He lifted Charlie's chin with his hand. "What do you say, we churn some vanilla ice cream to go with your mom's peanut butter and honey cookies?"

"Alright, dad!" Charlie replied excitedly, forgetting the bee sting for a moment. "Can we make it chocolate, instead?"

A few months later, Charlie turned five.

XIV

The following summer, when the clover blossomed again, Charlie could once more be found on his tummy with pencil and paper, drawing bees as they buzzed from blossom to blossom.

Charlie was older now. His drawings were better than those from the year before.

He waited patiently for a bee to land on a nearby blossom.

Sure enough, a bee landed on the blossom. Charlie began sketching the bee.

Before Charlie could finish his sketch, the bee flew away in search of other blossoms.

Charlie didn't mind, though. He knew other bees would come.

He no longer felt he needed to catch bees to draw them.

He could see them just fine the way they were.

The End

www.ingramcontent.com/pod-product-compliance
Lightning Source LLC
Chambersburg PA
CBHW070525290526
45790CB00003B/1299

* 9 7 8 1 5 0 2 5 0 7 3 3 4 *